Contents

What is a sports bat?

A bat is used to play a game.

The bowler throws the ball.

Material Detectives: Wood

Let's Look at a Sports Bat

Angela Royston

www.raintreepublishers.co.uk
Visit our website to find out more information about **Raintree** books.

To order:
☎ Phone 44 (0) 1865 888112
▤ Send a fax to 44 (O) 1865 314091
▢ Visit the Raintree Bookshop at **www.raintreepublishers**.co.uk to browse our catalogue and order online.

First published in Great Britain by Raintree, Halley Court, Jordan Hill, Oxford OX2 8EJ, part of Harcourt Education.
Raintree is a registered trademark of Harcourt Education Ltd.

Editorial: Andrew Farrow and Sarah Chappelow
Design: Jo Malivoire and AMR
Picture Research: Erica Newbery
Production: Duncan Gilbert

Originated by Modern Age
Printed and bound in China by South China Printing Company

10 digit ISBN 1 844 43637 3 (hardback)
13 digit ISBN 978 1 844 43637 8 (hardback)
10 09 08 07 06
10 9 8 7 6 5 4 3 2 1

10 digit ISBN 1 844 43642 X (paperback)
13 digit ISBN 978 1 844 43642 2 (paperback)
11 10 09 08 07
10 9 8 7 6 5 4 3 2 1

British Library Cataloguing in Publication Data
Royston, Angela
Wood: let's look at a sports bat. – (Material Detectives)
620.1'2
A full catalogue record for this book is available from the British Library

Acknowledgements
The publishers would like to thank the following for permission to reproduce photographs:
Alamy/Banana Stock p. 6; Banana Stock/Alamy p. 12; Brand X Pictures/Alamy p. 16; Harcourt Education p. 5; Image 100/Alamy pp. backcover (ball), 10; Ron Chapple/Alamy p. 4; Tudor Photography/Harcourt Education Ltd pp. backcover (stone), 7, 8, 9, 11, 13, 14, 15, 17, 18, 19, 20, 21, 22, 23 (all), 24.

Cover photograph of baseball bats reproduced with permission of Jim Cornfield/Corbis.

Every effort has been made to contact copyright holders of any material reproduced in this book. Any omissions will be rectified in subsequent printings if notice is given to the publishers.

The paper used to print this book comes from sustainable resources.

Some words are shown in bold, **like this**. You can find them in the glossary on page 23.

The batter tries to hit the ball with the bat.

What does a bat look like?

This bat is long and round.

It is easy to hold.

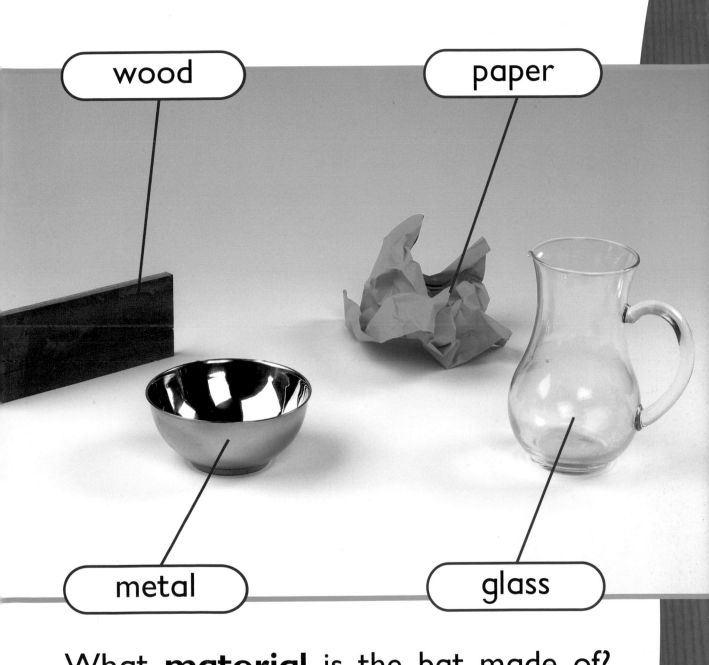

wood

paper

metal

glass

What **material** is the bat made of?

A bat is made of wood.

Can you see the patterns in this wood?

Wood can be **carved** into many different shapes.

These things are made of wood too.

Is a bat heavy or light?

A wooden bat is quite heavy.

It can hit a ball hard.

Is a wooden bat heavier or lighter than a plastic bat?

Wood is heavier than plastic.

You use two hands to swing a wooden sports bat.

Wood is lighter than stone.

A bat made of stone would be too heavy to pick up.

Is a bat rough or smooth?

Some wood is **rough**.

Rough wood can give you a splinter — be careful!

A wooden bat is rubbed and polished to make the wood smooth.

Is a bat hard or soft?

A bat is hard.

The ball bounces off the hard surface of the bat.

A ball does not bounce off a cushion.

This is because the cushion is soft.

Is a bat bendy or rigid?

Can you bend a sports bat?

No, a bat is strong and **rigid**.

A bat is more rigid than a **hosepipe**.

A hosepipe is bendy.

Do sports bats rot?

Some wood rots if it gets wet.

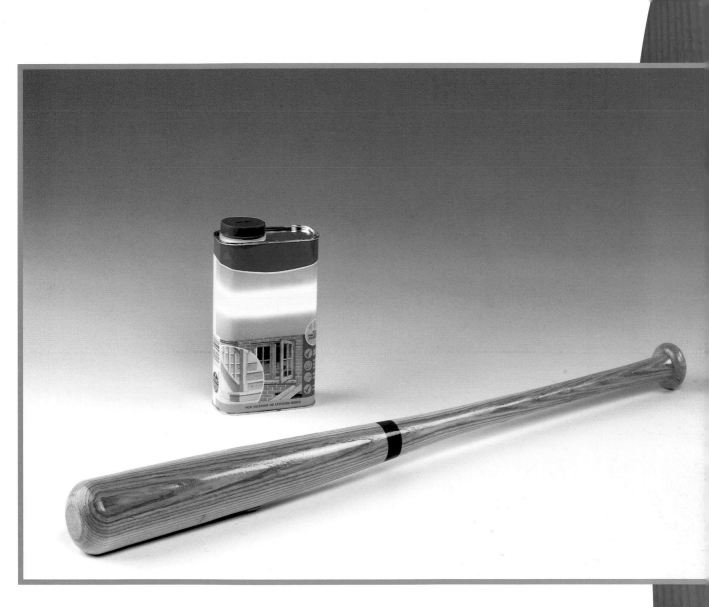

A sports bat does not rot.

The wood has been soaked in special **chemicals**.

Quiz

Which of these things are hard like a sports bat?

Which of them are soft?

Look for the answer on page 24.

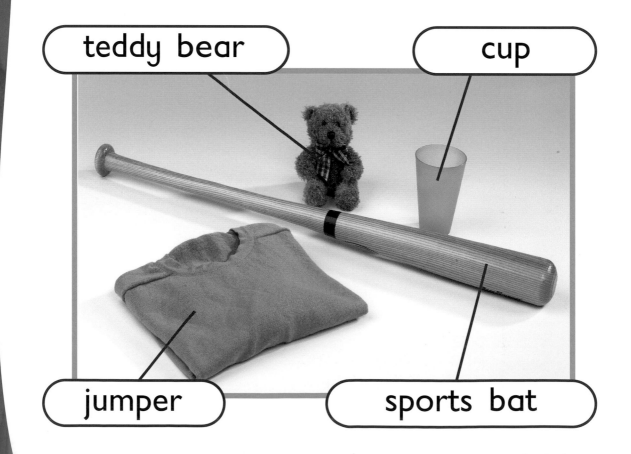

teddy bear

cup

jumper

sports bat

Glossary

carved
cut

chemicals
different kinds of things that make materials

hosepipe
tube that carries water from a tap

material
stuff that something is made of

rigid
stiff and hard to bend

rough
bumpy and uneven

Index

Answers to quiz on page 22

The bat and the cup are hard.

The teddy bear and the jumper are soft.

Note to parents and teachers

Reading for information is an important part of a child's literacy development. Learning begins with a question about something. Help children think of themselves as investigators and researchers by encouraging their questions about the world around them. Each chapter in this book begins with a question. Read the question together. Look at the pictures. Talk about what you think the answer might be. Then read the text to find out if your predictions were correct. Think of other questions you could ask about the topic, and discuss where you might find the answers. Assist children in using the picture glossary and the index to practice new vocabulary and research skills.